WELCOME TO THE HEART OF NEOLITHIC ORKNEY

The Neolithic remains on Orkney's Mainland make it a very special place indeed. Nowhere else in northern Europe can you visit a combination of 5,000-year-old villages alongside the spectacular ritual and burial monuments created by their inhabitants. The modern farming landscape abounds with these exceptionally well-preserved ancient monuments, and much more besides.

The Heart of Neolithic Orkney became a World Heritage Site in 1999, a mark of its international significance. It lies in the west of the largest of the Orkney Islands – George Mackay Brown's 'islands of stone' – 9 miles (15km) from the north-eastern tip of mainland Scotland. The concept of The Heart of Neolithic Orkney is a modern one, but the area was clearly regarded as an important place in the past. Its distinctive qualities – the setting of sea, lochs and the natural amphitheatre of hills, the wildlife and the sound, light and smell – amplify the visitor's experience as much as they did five millennia ago.

Above: Sunset behind the chambered tomb of Maeshowe, one of the greatest architectural achievements of Neolithic Britain.

CONTENTS

Left: Looking south-east from the Ring of Brodgar to the Stones of Stenness.

THE HEART OF NEOLITHIC ORKNEY AT A GLANCE

The Neolithic and Early Bronze Age monuments that form the World Heritage Site date from between 5,100 to 3,500 years ago. They include Maeshowe chambered tomb and the Barnhouse Stone; the Stones of Stenness stone circle and henge and Watchstone; the Ring of Brodgar stone circle, henge, adjacent standing stone and burial mounds; and Skara Brae village. All these sites, which are in state care, sit within a wider, multi-period archaeological landscape that includes another Neolithic settlement which you can also visit at Barnhouse. Many other sites are on private land.

Our tour will show you the highlights. Skara Brae has its own guidebook, so our focus is the Maeshowe and Brodgar area. We will also join the dots in an exploration of the wider landscape, aided by the latest archaeological discoveries and ideas.

Right: Part of the massive stone circle at the Ring of Brodgar, believed to have been built for ritual religious purposes. Like other Neolithic monuments on Orkney, the Ring testifies to an early and sophisticated society in northern Britain.

MONUMENTAL CREATIONS

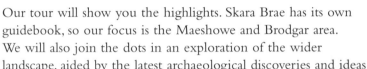

SOPHISTICATED HOMES

COMPLEX BELIEFS

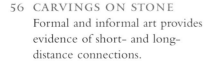
THE PULL OF THE PLACE

A GUIDED TOUR

Our ancestors travelled on foot – and later horseback – along beaches and across heaths, bogs and fields. Small timber and skin boats carried them over the water. Today we drive, bus, cycle or walk along formal routes, all of which influence how we approach and experience the sites. You can, however, visit the monuments that make up the Heart of Neolithic Orkney in any order you choose, and often from different directions (although there is a logic to visiting Barnhouse before the Stones of Stenness). The sites naturally fall into two groups: the Maeshowe area and Skara Brae. The map opposite shows where you can park and what land is open to the public.

Walking is a good way to appreciate how the monuments sit in the landscape. Check locally for updates on the extent of the footpath network and car park locations, as well as details of public transport. And please remember to respect land in private ownership and to follow the Scottish Outdoor Access Code (www.outdooraccess-scotland.com).

You only pay to visit Maeshowe and Skara Brae, and must pre-book for Maeshowe. The other sites are open at all times, and Historic Scotland's Ranger Service offers free guided walks.

Right: (main image)
One of the standing stones at the Stones of Stenness; **(1)** an entranceway at Skara Brae village; **(2)** the reconstructed dwellings at Barnhouse village; **(3)** the Stones of Stenness, with the Loch of Stenness in the foreground; **(4)** standing stones at the Ring of Brodgar; **(5)** the Watchstone, standing to the north-west of the Stones of Stenness; **(6)** Maeshowe; and **(7)** the Barnhouse Stone, which directly aligns with the entrance to Maeshowe, 800m to the north-east.

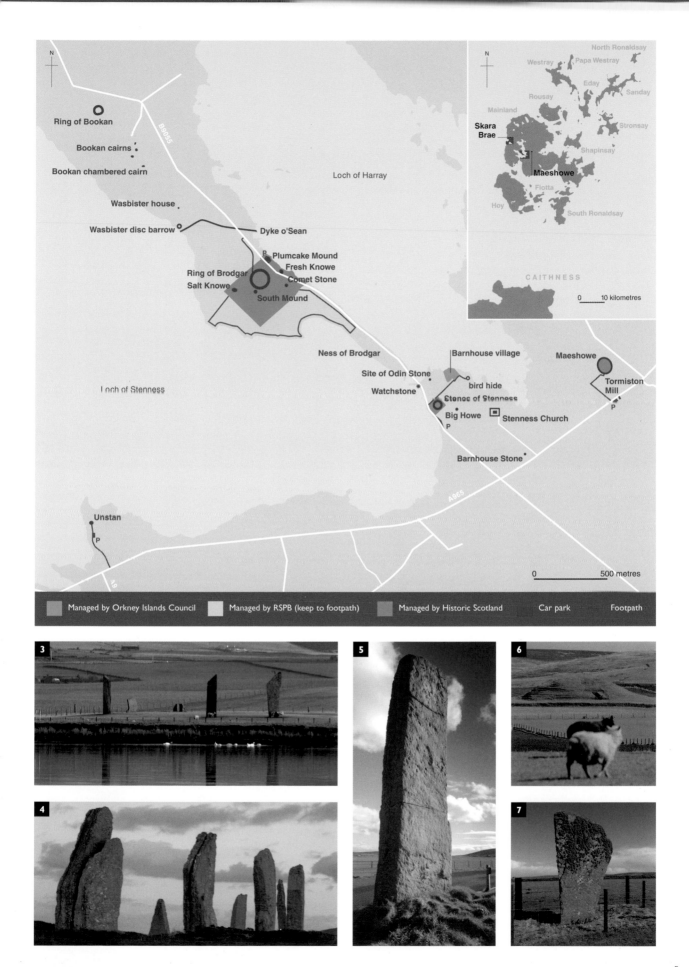

Ring of Bookan

Bookan cairns

Bookan chambered cairn

Loch of Harray

B9055

Wasbister house

Wasbister disc barrow

Dyke o'Sean

Plumcake Mound

Fresh Knowe

Ring of Brodgar

Comet Stone

Salt Knowe

South Mound

Ness of Brodgar

Barnhouse village

Maeshowe

Loch of Stenness

Site of Odin Stone

bird hide

Tormiston Mill

Watchstone

Stones of Stenness

Big Howe

Stenness Church

Barnhouse Stone

A965

Unstan

North Ronaldsay

Westray

Papa Westray

Rousay

Eday

Sanday

Mainland

Stronsay

Skara Brae

Shapinsay

Maeshowe

Flotta

Hoy

South Ronaldsay

CAITHNESS

0   10 kilometres

0   500 metres

Managed by Orkney Islands Council   Managed by RSPB (keep to footpath)   Managed by Historic Scotland   Car park   Footpath

THE NEOLITHIC LANDSCAPE

Below: Neolithic people used flint cutting tools such as this for a variety of tasks, including the preparation of animal skins.

W e do not know for sure when the first people arrived in Orkney – perhaps about 8,500 years ago. Just as today, these settlers would have found an environment rich in natural resources. Early Orcadians were hunter-gatherers, who moved from place to place, living off seasonally available plants, as well as hunting and fishing. Discoveries of flint tools provide glimpses into how these people worked and survived.

Knowledge of farming techniques arrived about 5,500 years ago. By this time the vegetation would probably have been mainly grassland and heath, with patches of scrubby birch and hazel. In 2003 archaeologists found the first signs of Neolithic timber structures at Wideford (to the west of Kirkwall), potentially the earliest houses in Orkney. This leads us to suspect that there were stands of well-grown trees in some sheltered spots. But all the evidence points to Orkney having lost most of its trees thousands of years ago.

The largely treeless landscape of Neolithic Orkney would have been populated by farms and villages interspersed with burial and ceremonial places. The surrounding land would have been a

mixture of small plots used for growing bere (a primitive form of barley) and wheat, pastoral grassland for grazing domesticated sheep and cattle, and heath.

A NATURAL AMPHITHEATRE

The Neolithic monuments which make up Orkney's World Heritage Site are located in low-lying land around the lochs of Stenness and Harray, surrounded by a natural amphitheatre of hills. It is likely that the land's natural bowl-shape provided added appeal for the monument builders – it is common in northern Britain to find clusters of late Neolithic monuments at such locations. Machrie Moor on Arran is another good example.

A short narrow isthmus runs between the two lochs, comprising two peninsulas, joined for at least 1,000 years by a bridge ('Brodgar' derives from the Old Norse Brúgarðr, meaning 'bridge farm'). In Neolithic times the waters of the lochs would have been lower than we find them, but there is no evidence that the two lochs were truly separate. So today, as in prehistory, the Loch of Stenness gives direct access to the open sea a short distance away. The Loch of Harray is now mainly freshwater, although more seawater would have flowed into it before 1968, when engineers altered the flow of water between the two lochs at the Bridge of Brodgar. We can only wonder how prehistoric peoples regarded this crossroads of land and sea, freshwater and brine.

Above: The mound of Maeshowe looms in the foreground of this view, with the narrow strip of land that runs between the freshwater Loch of Harray and the saltwater Loch of Stenness behind. The Watchstone standing stone is visible next to the cottage on the left-hand side; the Ring of Brodgar just discernible on the right (across the water from Maeshowe).

Every community on earth is being deprived of an ancient
necessary nourishment. We cannot live fully without the
treasury our ancestors have left us. Without the story –
in which everyone living, unborn, and dead participates –
men are no more than 'bits of paper blown on the cold wind…'

George Mackay Brown, *Winter Tales* (1995)

THE BIGGER PICTURE

The sites that form the Heart of Neolithic Orkney are only the tip of the iceberg. An extensive archaeological landscape survives beneath and between the monuments we can see, much of it invisible to the eye. The visible remains date from the Neolithic to the present day.

When visiting Orkney's World Heritage Site it is important to consider the landscape as more than a series of dots, or compartments of surviving monuments. Instead, try to imagine it as a tapestry into which the lives of humans, monuments and artefacts are interwoven. Think of a very old fabric, constantly reworked through time with losses, additions and repairs, and with the many people that worked on it each bringing their own memories and motivations to the task.

The story of human settlement involves a constant reworking of the environment, but some activities have a bigger impact than others. Orkney's smaller Neolithic sites, for example, have been more vulnerable to change, while settlements such as Barnhouse provided a ready supply of building stone for recycling. The ritual sites with their big banks, ditches and standing stones have often survived better, perhaps because later generations continued to respect them in some way. In the 19th and 20th centuries farming both reduced the number of monuments and changed the use of land on Orkney. Over the same period, antiquarians and archaeologists also altered the profile of monuments such as Maeshowe through excavation.

UNPICKING THE PAST

The impact of all these activities is cumulative. Our challenge is to unpick each 'stitch' in the landscape and to understand society through time, while caring for the evidence that survives. We will never know the full truth about what happened in the past, but we constantly edge towards better and more subtle understandings. Our ability to do this is dependent on the nature, quality and extent of our observations and the way in which we interpret them.

We must use our imagination to look at familiar things in new ways, and to think outside of our 21st-century perspective. Only by doing this can we approach the question that all the monuments in Orkney's World Heritage Site demand of us: how did people experience their real and imagined worlds 5,000 years ago?

Left: An aerial view looking south-west from the Ring of Brodgar, with the Loch of Stenness behind. Beyond lie the sheltered waters of Scapa Flow, with the Hills of Hoy on the horizon.

MAESHOWE

Maeshowe is the finest chambered tomb in north-west Europe. It consists of a grassy mound that sits on a large circular platform surrounded by a ditch and, beyond this, a bank. The mound contains a long stone passage – tombs like Maeshowe are often called passage graves – leading to an elaborate, stone-lined chamber with side cells. 'Howe' derives from the Old Norse for a hill, but the origin of 'Maes' is less clear.

Maeshowe is dated to around 5,000 years ago because of its form and relationship to better-dated tombs and settlements. Our only scientifically obtained data tells us that the ditch was dug more than 4,500 years ago.

Below: Snow carpets Maeshowe in this aerial view, emphasising the platform on which the mound sits, the ditch beyond and the encircling wall.

BUILT TO IMPRESS

Our ancestors designed Maeshowe to make an impact.
Many hands carried stones and clay to build the mound and
excavate the ditch – all without the aid of metal tools or
powered machinery. There is no doubt that its construction
was a major enterprise and a tremendous social commitment.
One challenge when visiting Maeshowe is to link what you
discover inside the tomb to what lies outside it. You are sure
to be awed by its atmosphere, as well as the Neolithic building
skills and the Norse runes, but spare some time for the rest of
the monument, and its relationship to the landscape.

Above: The 10m-long entrance
passage into Maeshowe.
Maeshowe was a masterpiece in
Neolithic design and stonework
construction, not least for its use
of massive individual stones,
which can be seen here forming
the passage walls, floor and roof.

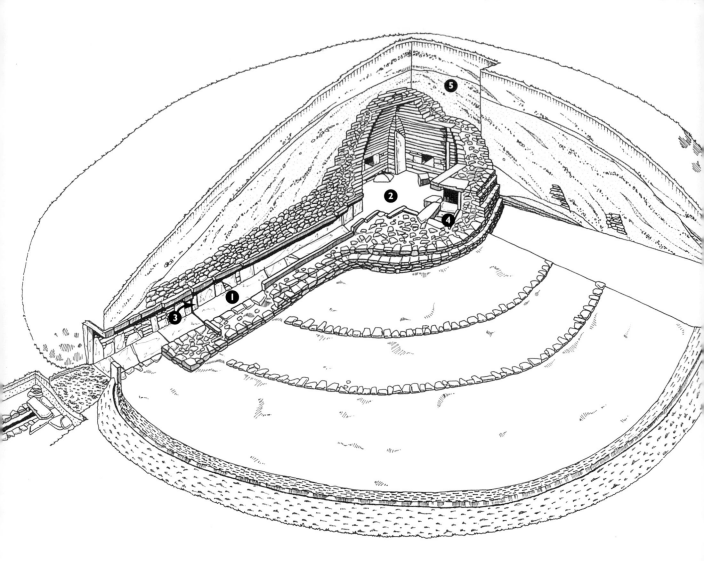

BUILDING MAESHOWE

The construction of Maeshowe is deceptively complex. The insights we have into its design come from a series of small-scale excavations, the first of which took place in Victorian times. More recently, archaeologists explored Maeshowe in the 1950s, the 1970s and the early 1990s. The 1990s excavations revealed that the mound is not the earliest Neolithic structure on the site. Archaeologists digging in front of the entrance to the tomb discovered a 'drain' that seems to relate to an earlier building, possibly a house.

THE DITCH, PLATFORM AND BANK

The Neolithic builders may have dug the ditch before constructing the mound – but we do not know this for certain. The ditch is, in fact, a very clever sculpting of a natural glacial mound to enhance the appearance of the site. To form it, the builders cut the rock around three-quarters of the sub-circular platform on which the mound sits to create a flat-bottomed

Above: The passageway (**1**) and main chamber (**2**) were carefully constructed to align towards the setting sun at midwinter, while the large blocking stone (**3**) could seal off the tomb when necessary. The walls of the chamber are formed of flagstones, grading towards the roof. Side cells (**4**) come off the main chamber, which is surrounded by stone walls and a thick layer of clay and stones (**5**).

feature. The ditch would have been about 0.7m deeper than it is today, and possibly held water. An encircling ditch like this around a passage grave is exceptionally rare, and it is not clear how our ancestors would have crossed it.

Around the circuit of the platform was at least one sizeable standing stone. In the 1990s, archaeologists found the stone hole, but no evidence for a stone circle. Further away from the mound, underneath the modern enclosing turf bank, is evidence of an outer stone wall that seems to be contemporary with the ditch. Its original height is unknown, but it could have been substantial.

THE MOUND

The mound itself is about 35m across and 7m high. The central chamber is encased by a well-built corbelled wall that grades in height towards the roof. Beyond this wall are two low, encircling stone retaining walls. A thick layer of clay and small stones, sealed by a clay skin now covered with green turf, seals the whole. The builders used yellow clay at Maeshowe, which they probably carried in baskets from the lochside.

The end result is a carefully crafted, robust and watertight structure to which people could control access. Its present soft, rounded exterior masks a starkly different interior space, where darkness and the straight lines of stones predominate. When first built, the cut rock, clay capping and stone encircling wall may have lessened this contrast.

Below: Maeshowe guards its secrets well. We do not know, for instance, whether the mound was originally covered with turf, as it is today. Moreover, while excavations have revealed that the tomb sits on top of an earlier monument, we can only guess at the purpose of this earlier building.

MAESHOWE: INSIDE THE TOMB

Inside the tomb at Maeshowe we feel quite remote from the outside world, and our senses are alert to the qualities of the space. In contrast to the massive mound around us, we are in a small room measuring only 4.7m across and 4.5m high (the original height was possibly as much as 6m). Behind us only a small glint of daylight beckons.

This daylight comes from the 10m-long entrance passage, a gently rising paved corridor. Inside the passage is a recess containing a large wedge-shaped stone, balanced on a pivot, which those inside could twist across to seal the tomb. Forming most of each wall of the passage is a single, gigantic sandstone slab, the largest weighing about three tonnes.

THE SIDE CELLS AND ROOF

We enter the tomb from the centre of one wall. At the mid-point of each of the other three walls is an elevated side chamber, or cell. Two of the three cells contain a low platform (the third may also have done so originally). The floor, back wall and ceiling of the cells are single stones.

The roof of the main chamber is a corbelled vault, most of whose slabs span the complete wall width. Its top was removed when the curious Norse and, much later, Victorians broke into the mound, prompting the then owner of Maeshowe, a Mr Balfour, to build a roof over it in the early 1860s. Shortly after 1910, when the monument came into state care, an invisible concrete slab was added above the roof.

Right: The modern 'discovery' of Maeshowe began with James Farrer and other antiquarians, who broke into the mound in 1861. Farrer's drawing is useful on many counts, not the least of which is to show the technique of corbelling (laying overlapping stones on top of each other) which the Neolithic builders used to form the roof.

Opposite page: (main image)
The main chamber at Maeshowe, with the passageway leading into the south-west wall. The side cells built into the south-east (left) and north-west (right) walls are visible, as are two of the four stone uprights. **(1)** The blocking stone part-way along the passageway, housed in a specially designed recess. **(2)** Neolithic people scored Maeshowe's walls with pick marks, as well as incising abstract designs, such as this one.

STONE UPRIGHTS

At each corner of the main chamber is a magnificent upright, a standing stone encased within a pier, or corner-block of smaller stones. These uprights dictated the height of the roof at Maeshowe, but did not have a structural function. Standing proud as the tomb was built around them, it is possible that they first stood elsewhere on the site. They cannot, however, have been exposed to the elements for long because the stone remains fresh and unweathered.

Perhaps the stones that now line the passage were also originally standing stones; in scale they compare to the largest uprights at the Stones of Stenness. Maeshowe is the only passage grave known to incorporate standing stones, but the idea could stem from the tradition of earlier Neolithic stalled cairns, such as those at Unstan or Midhowe. These contain a line of paired upright stones which were gradually encased within the body of the cairn.

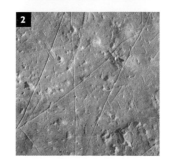

STOOP THROUGH THE
LONG NARROW CORRIDOR
TOWARDS THE CHAMBER OF
DARKNESS, WINTER, DEATH.

George Mackay Brown, 'Maeshowe at
Midwinter' in *Under Brinkie's Brae* (1979)

BURIALS AT MAESHOWE

Archaeologists believe that Maeshowe was used for communal burials, but this conclusion is far from straightforward. The tomb has been disturbed so many times in the past, and its clearance in the 19th century was not scientifically carried out. As a result, the only recorded finds are fragments of human skull and some horse bones, now lost.

We can infer that Maeshowe was a tomb from the better excavation of related monuments. Of these, Quanterness, 6 miles (10km) east of Maeshowe, is our best comparison. Here, archaeologists found the remains of more than 157 individuals of all ages, and estimate that it could have originally held the remains of around 400 people. Other tombs held smaller populations.

THE BONES OF THE DEAD

Neolithic people selected bones to bring to tombs, which they appear to have rearranged or cleared out regularly. This practice means that bodies had to be defleshed somewhere, and the bones subsequently collected. In some parts of south-east Scotland, discoveries of post-holes have been interpreted as the remains of timber mortuary platforms on which bodies might be exposed until the bones could be collected. There could have been equivalent structures on or around Orkney's chambered tombs, or perhaps in the lochs. Another possibility is that the early Orcadians buried their dead and dug them up after the flesh had rotted.

We might imagine a scenario, then, in which at certain times of the year select members of the community gathered the bones of their dead, ceremonially brought them into Maeshowe and carefully arranged them on the platforms or 'beds' in the side cells. They might regularly bring their ancestors' bones in and out of the tomb, reuniting the inside and outside worlds, accompanied by offerings of pottery and other goods. At some point, the side cells were sealed with well-fitting stones.

Above: The side cells at Maeshowe may have served as the repositories of the bones of the dead.

Opposite: Neolithic Orcadians may have used Maeshowe, silhouetted here by the setting sun, to house the bones of members of the local community. Like other tombs, Maeshowe was designed to be entered and re-entered – a place for the living as well as the dead.

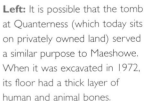

Left: It is possible that the tomb at Quanterness (which today sits on privately owned land) served a similar purpose to Maeshowe. When it was excavated in 1972, its floor had a thick layer of human and animal bones.

MIDWINTER AT MAESHOWE

We do know that one time of year was particularly special for the people who used Maeshowe. The gently sloping passageway into the tomb is carefully aligned so that at sunset during the three weeks before and after the shortest day of the year (21st December) the light of the setting sun shines straight down the passage and illuminates the back of the chamber. The sun's rays align with a standing stone, the Barnhouse Stone, standing 800m south–south-west of Maeshowe itself.

Opposite: The Barnhouse Stone, with Maeshowe behind. At midwinter the sunlight directly aligns with the Barnhouse Stone before passing down the passageway at Maeshowe.

Below: The setting midwinter sun illuminates the back wall of the chamber at Maeshowe.

THE TORCH IS PLUCKED FROM
THE DYING HANDS OF THE YEAR:
A NEW TIME HAS BEGUN.

George Mackay Brown, *Portrait of Orkney* (1981)

It seems, therefore, that cycles of life and death were linked to the annual cycle of the seasons – the death of one year and the birth of another. Alignment with aspects of the winter or summer solstices is also a feature of some other Neolithic passage graves. It is sometimes difficult to distinguish between the significance of solar and lunar events, and in fact the latter cannot be ruled out for Maeshowe because of the long period over which the chamber is lit.

Another passage grave illuminated by winter solstice sunlight is Newgrange, in Ireland's Boyne Valley. Unlike at Maeshowe, the rising midwinter sun lights Newgrange's chamber. For one day only, a carefully designed light box channels the sun's rays through the body of the cairn above the passageway. At Maeshowe, in contrast, celebrants may have pivoted a massive stone to seal the entrance, leaving a gap at the top of 47cm. This practice could have intensified the midwinter experience for those inside.

Above: The Neolithic builders of the chambered tomb at Newgrange in Ireland designed it, like Maeshowe, to channel the midwinter sun's rays along its passageway.

MAESHOWE: THE NORSE DISCOVERY

I t seems that after several hundred years of use as a burial chamber, beliefs changed and Maeshowe was closed up. At least 3,000 years passed before it again attracted any significant interest that archaeologists have been able to detect. Then, in the middle of the 12th century AD, the Norse – descendants of the Vikings – broke into the mound. As a testament of their discovery they left light-hearted carvings all over the walls of the tomb, in the form of at least 33 runic inscriptions and eight sketches. This graffiti comprises the largest collection of runic inscriptions that survive outside Scandinavia – a potent reminder that Orkney was under Norwegian rule until 1468.

From the late 8th century pagan Vikings from Norway were raiding in Scotland. They settled in Orkney, establishing a semi-independent Norse earldom and a staging post on the major trading route between Ireland and Scandinavia. By the 12th century, Orkney was a place of considerable cultural achievements. Kirkwall was by then flourishing as an urban centre, and in 1137 work began on its splendid Romanesque cathedral, dedicated to St Magnus. Orkney's Norse earls, by now Christian, were wealthy and well travelled, with extensive connections. The early 13th-century Orkneyinga Saga tells their story. It is here that Maeshowe get its first mention in surviving written sources, and here too that we learn of at least one occasion when the Norse visited the tomb.

Above: Norse carved heads on the walls of St Magnus Cathedral, Kirkwall. The cathedral was built at around the same time that the Norse broke into Maeshowe.

Right: An illustration of the south-east wall of the chamber at Maeshowe, showing the location of runic inscriptions. A selection of the inscriptions – either whole or in part – is shown alongside, together with translations of each one that appears on this wall.

ORKAHAUGR

The Norse knew Maeshowe by a different name. Shortly after Christmas 1153, Earl Harald Maddadarson and 100 men were travelling from Hamnavoe (Stromness) to Firth (the Finstown area). Caught in a snowstorm, they took shelter in 'Orkahaugr'. Two inscriptions in the tomb use the name of 'Orkahaugr', and its location fits the story as described in the Orkneyinga Saga. Maeshowe is also the only 'haugr' (howe) that we know the Norse broke into. The implication is that the tomb was already accessible and the properties of its interior familiar.

References in the runes to Jerusalem-travellers or pilgrims tell us that the Norse entered Maeshowe on at least one other occasion. The Orkneyinga Saga mentions how Earl Rognvald gathered his men together in 1150–51. They travelled first to Rome and then Jerusalem, as pilgrims, returning late in 1153 after many adventures. Rognvald is probably the earl to whom the (female) cook Lif refers in her carving. The pilgrims give themselves the credit for breaking into the tomb, and it seems most likely that they first did so before they left, if Harald and his men were able to get into it in 1153.

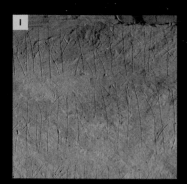

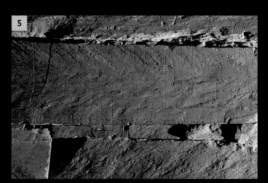

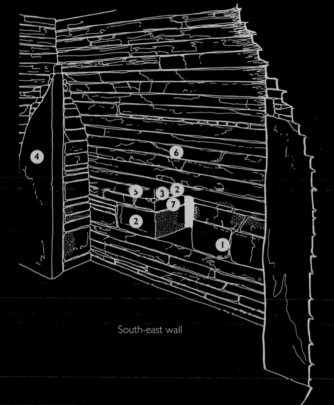

South-east wall

1 'This mound was built before Lothbrok's. Her sons, they were bold; such were men, as they were of themselves [i.e. they were the sort of people you could really call men]. Jerusalem-travellers broke Orkhaugr. Lif, the Earl's housekeeper, carved. In the north-west great treasure is hidden. It was long ago that great treasure was hidden here. Happy is he who can find the great wealth. Hakon alone carried treasure out of this mound. Simon. Sigrith.' In this group of individual carvings men and women banter with each other in a light-hearted manner.

2 'The man who is most skilled in runes west of the ocean carved these runes with the axe which Gauk Trandilsson owned in the south of the country [Iceland].' Two different types of runes are used here.

3 'Ingigerth is the most beautiful…' The sketch of a slavering dog next to this inscription suggests an appreciation of Ingigerth's charms.

4 'Ofram Sigurdsson carved these runes.' This carving came away from the wall after its 19th-century discovery. It is notable for its cluster of crosses, although these do not prove that Ofram was a pilgrim.

5 'Hermund hard … carved runes.'

6 'Arnfinn food carved these runes.' Several of the inscriptions appear to include nicknames, so perhaps Arnfinn was a greedy man.

7 'Benedikt made this cross.' We do not know which of the crosses within the tomb this refers to.

1 'I 'fuþorkhniastbynu.' A version of the runic alphabet used at Maeshowe.

2 'Ingibiorg the fair widow. Many a woman has gone stooping in here. A great show-off. Erling.' Does this mean that all or part of the passage to the tomb was open at this time? The Norse selected flat surfaces to work on, usually avoiding the areas of Neolithic pick-marking. Here, however, you can see a band of pecking underneath the inscription.

3 'That will be true which I say, that treasure was carried away. Treasure was carried away three nights before they broke this mound.'

4 '…is told to me that treasure is hidden here well enough. Few say as Odd Orkason said in those runes which he cut.'

5 'Thorni bedded. Helgi carved.'

6 'Eyjolf Kolbeinsson carved these runes high.' A lot of effort went into achieving this boast!

7 'That is a Viking…then came underneath to this place.'

8 'Otarr…carved these runes.'

9 'Vemund carved.'

10 'Thorir…'

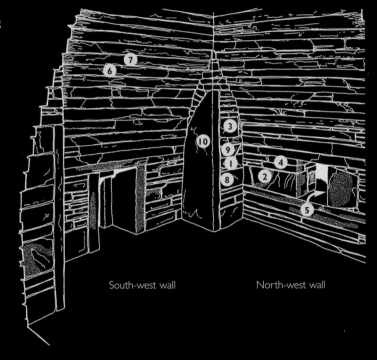

South-west wall   North-west wall

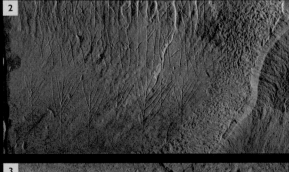

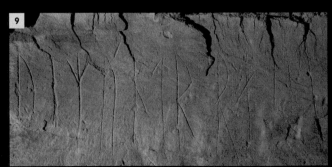

MAESHOWE: UNDERSTANDING THE RUNES

The angular letters used in Maeshowe belong to runic alphabets developed by Germanic peoples from the 2nd century AD. Derived in part from the Roman alphabet, these letters could be cut quickly onto stone, wood or bone. We find them used for inscriptions, graffiti, everyday messages and magical formulae.

The standard runic alphabet as used by the 12th-century Norse consisted of 16 letters: fuþork – hnias – tbmlR (þ, thorn, is written out as th). On the south-west wall of the tomb one person carved the fuþork alphabet (as it is known), although they muddled the last three letters: In fact, a fuller range of letters is used at Maeshowe:

TWIG RUNES

If the Norse wanted to be clever or to tease their readers they wrote in cryptic twig runes. For example, one inscriber called Erling signed his name in twig runes on the north-west wall, while on the south-east the man 'most skilled in runes west of the ocean' showed off by beginning in twig runes and progressing to standard runes.

INTERPRETING THE RUNES

It is one thing to know the runic characters, but quite another thing to work out which letters are represented on the walls of the tomb, and to make sense of what they say in Old Norse. Sometimes this is straightforward, but we are left with gaps and uncertainties, particularly when the inscriptions are worn. Often the translations can be, at best, tentative.

Above: A detail from carving 2 (see opposite page). The Norse at Maeshowe used standard runes as well as twig runes to carve their messages. Sometimes, as in this inscription, they used both.

Opposite page: An illustration of the south-west and north-west walls, showing the location of runic inscriptions, a selection of the inscriptions themselves – either whole or in part – and translations of each one that appears on these walls.

Left: Use the table on the left to decipher twig runes. Count the branches on either side of each rune and read the left-hand column on the table first. The twig runes next to the table correspond to 'ærlikr', which we can interpret as 'Erling'.

MAESHOWE: ABLE MINDS AND PRACTISED HANDS?

The Norse inscribers of Maeshowe carved with knives or other sharp implements. The neatness of the inscriptions varies, but they clearly demonstrate that their male and female inscribers were to some degree literate. As well as being witty and skilled in carving runes, some of the men and women who entered Maeshowe were also artistic. The 'Maeshowe lion', commonly known as a dragon, demonstrates this ability. Beneath the lion is an indeterminate animal (a walrus, otter or seal) and a knotted serpent or snake. Lion graffiti is common in Romanesque Scandinavia, but we do not know how symbolic the choice of this image was.

TALES OF TREASURE

Norse inscriptions on three sides of the tomb contain references to treasure. What do such references mean? To examine this question we must turn our minds to what the Norse would have found when they broke into the tomb. We do not know what the Neolithic people left in the tomb when they finally closed it, but it is possible that the sealed side cells would have contained human bones, as well as pottery or stone tools. We also do not know if anyone entered the tomb before the Norse and, if so, what they disturbed. But we are confident that prehistoric peoples would have left nothing that the Norse would have regarded as treasure.

Some people have wondered whether pagan Vikings might have reused the tomb for the burial of one of their leaders in the 9th or 10th century. Fine metalwork could accompany such burials, and would certainly have constituted 'treasure' for any Norse who came across it several centuries later. However, while we cannot rule this possibility out, there is no evidence to support it. The idea stemmed from a radiocarbon dating of peat used to heighten the bank around the ditch at Maeshowe. The test dated the peat to the 9th century, but this only provides a date for the source of the peat, and not the works to the bank.

Instead, we need to imagine what the Norse who rediscovered the tomb would have felt – the impact of this dark and wondrous cavern. Storytelling was an important part of Norse life, and 'Orkahaugr' clearly developed its own mythology and an important place in Orcadian folklore, as its mention in the Orkneyinga Saga suggests. It cannot have been long after the early 13th century, the time of the saga's composition, that Maeshowe's roof collapsed, thereby sealing the tomb and its Norse graffiti.

Above: Norse people's skill with runes was matched by their artistic achievements, as this late-12th century chess piece of a warrior shows. The figure is part of a superb set of pieces, carved from walrus ivory and discovered in a stone box in a sand dune in Uig, Lewis.

Right: An illustration of the north-east wall, showing the location of runic inscriptions, a selection of the inscriptions themselves – either whole or in part – and translations of each one that appears on the wall.

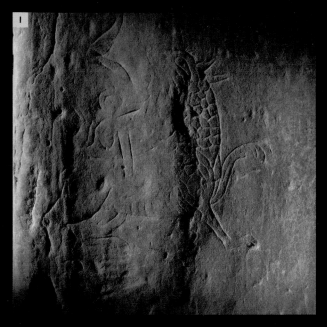

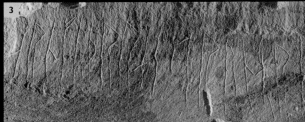

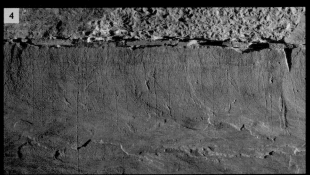

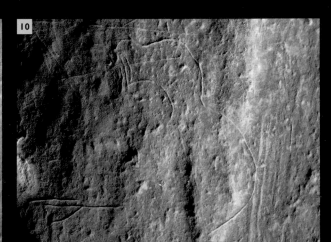

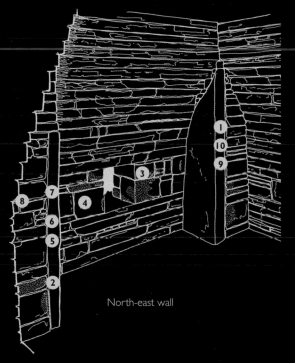

North-east wall

1 The 'Maeshowe lion', or dragon, dates on stylistic grounds to just before AD 1150. Its design combines Romanesque and late Viking features.

2 'Jerusalem men broke this mound.'

3 'Arnfinn, son of Steinn, carved these runes.'

4 '…carved these runes.' The form of runes used here is unparalleled anywhere else.

5 'Orm the…carved.' Orm was perhaps 'the younger'.

6 'Ogmund carved…'

7 This was probably a name, but no text suggests itself.

8 This consists of a number of vertical lines — possibly the initial stage in the carving of a runic inscription.

9 A knotted serpent or snake.

10 An indeterminate animal (possibly a walrus, otter or seal), as well as some individual runic letters.

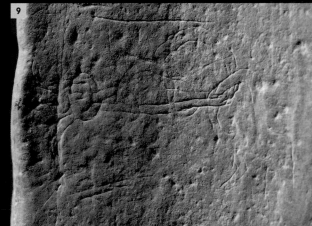

BARNHOUSE VILLAGE

In 1984 the archaeologist Colin Richards discovered and subsequently excavated a settlement 200m north–north-east of the Stones of Stenness. This discovery, of the foundations of a Late Neolithic village, was one of the most important archaeological finds in Britain in the late 20th century.

Understanding Barnhouse helps us to interpret what we see at the other sites. The people who lived in the village, from around 5,100 to 4,800 years ago onwards, probably built and frequented the Stones of Stenness, Maeshowe and possibly even the Ring of Brodgar. They could also have known people who lived at Skara Brae.

What you see at Barnhouse is a modern reconstruction of the foundations of four of the excavated buildings. This represents only a part of the settlement, and the buildings visible today are from different phases of building. Timber uprights indicate where archaeologists found stone sockets for wooden posts that might relate to internal divisions or furniture. The intention is that you can gain an impression of both scale and layout.

Below: The reconstructed site of Structure 8 at Barnhouse, with the Stones of Stenness in the background. Evidence from the remains of up to 14 buildings at Barnhouse suggests that while most were dwelling places, some – notably Structure 8 – served other purposes.

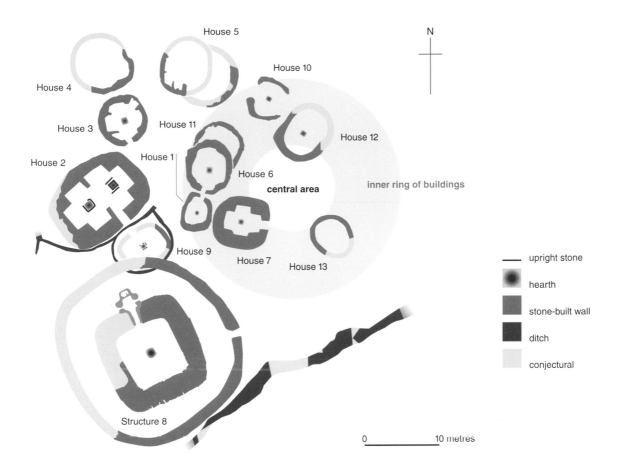

House 5

House 10

House 4

House 11

House 3

House 1

House 12

House 2

House 6

central area

inner ring of buildings

House 9

House 7

House 13

Structure 8

N

upright stone

◆ hearth

stone-built wall

ditch

conjectural

0 _____ 10 metres

DEVELOPMENT OF THE VILLAGE

Barnhouse village was not the first example of
activity in the Maeshowe area. A Neolithic tomb
at Unstan predates the site, as does a possible house
beneath Maeshowe itself (see page 12). The remains
of earlier farmsteads, villages and farms also lie under
the present-day fields, as at Stonehall and Wideford
to the east.

When it was established, the community at
Barnhouse grew quickly. Archaeologists have
excavated the remains of up to 14 buildings.
Because the stratigraphy (archaeological layers) is
so shallow, it is difficult to phase these well, but a
monumental building, known as Structure 8, is last
in the sequence. Each of the buildings experienced
many phases of reworking and rebuilding, while
between and around them mounds of midden
(rubbish) and decayed roofing materials built up.

Above top: A plan summarising the settlement
evidence from Barnhouse.

Above: An artist's impression of how Barnhouse
village may have looked when inhabited. The
suggestion that the roofs consisted of wooden
frames thatched with seaweed comes from the
evidence of later buildings in the Northern Isles.

BARNHOUSE VILLAGE: UNDERSTANDING THE BUILDINGS

L ike the dwellings at Skara Brae, the houses uncovered at Barnhouse have central hearths, stone furniture and recessed spaces. Two buildings, however – House 2 and Structure 8 – stand out from the others. Their differences suggest that they served ceremonial, rather than domestic, purposes.

Excavations at Barnhouse found signs that people had constructed houses on the same site a number times. At the heart of the village was an open area, where evidence suggests that inhabitants worked, for example preparing animal skins and fashioning clay into pots and other ware.

HOUSE 3

One of the earliest dwellings at Barnhouse, House 3 shares typical features with other Orcadian Late Neolithic houses. Its entrance – like that of around 80 per cent of such dwellings – is orientated from north-west to south-east, and leads into a square space with a central hearth. To the right and left of the hearth are large box features, while on the back wall is a 'dresser'. From a modern perspective it is easy to think of these features as beds and shelving, but we could well be wrong.

HOUSE 6

The orientation of House 6 is quite different from the others. Its plan and associated finds suggest that it had a specialist function. Unusually, its entrance is from the south-west. House 6 seems to have originally conformed to the typical cross-shaped arrangement of space, but this changed during its long occupation. While it may have been a house, the worked flints and pumice that archaeologists have found in its midden imply that the specialised working of bone, wood or hide took place here.

HOUSE 2

Built on a clay platform, House 2 is larger and more prominently sited than the other houses at Barnhouse. Its walls are of very high quality masonry – its builders clearly intended its exterior stonework to be seen – while its internal layout is far more complex than any of the other buildings. Unlike the other dwellings, House 2 was maintained throughout the occupation of the site.

The interior is two joined-up, cross-shaped spaces, which compare to the layout of passage graves such as Quoyness and Quanterness. The furniture in the eastern half dictated movement in an anti-clockwise direction. The western half is orientated differently. To enter this deeper section, inhabitants would have had to walk over a cist (box) containing animal or human bones. Cooking and eating took place in the eastern half, while the manufacture of stone maceheads seems to have taken place in the more secluded western half.

STRUCTURE 8

The form and scale of Structure 8, the last building to be completed at Barnhouse, suggests that it was not a house at all. Its builders developed it on the site of an earlier dwelling, removing the hearth of the former central area to create an internal floor space almost twice the size of that at Maeshowe. Like Maeshowe, a clay platform and a substantial stone wall surround Structure 8. While there is no evidence for domestic occupation, pottery finds suggest that plenty of food preparation took place on the surrounding platform.

At the entrance to the structure is an unusual porch arrangement that includes a fireplace at the threshold, similar to that at the Stones of Stenness. This, however, was unlikely to have been a visible feature once the building was completed. Similarities with the Stones of Stenness reinforce the notion that Structure 8 was used for rituals of some sort.

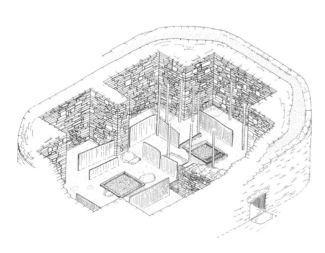

Above: A reconstruction of the inside of House 2.

Right: Excavating Structure 8.

THE STONES OF STENNESS

The great advantage of approaching the Stones of Stenness from Barnhouse village is that we follow in the footsteps of the people who built this ceremonial 'temple'. Our scientific dates for the construction of the site are frustratingly vague – from 5,400 to 4,500 years ago – but we can be reasonably confident that the two co-existed at some point, and the suggestion is that the Stones of Stenness appeared shortly after the village.

The standing stones would have looked very different when they were built and used than they do today. A considerable physical obstacle surrounded them – a henge, or ceremonial enclosure. This was a substantial outer bank (of unknown dimensions) and an inner waterlogged ditch (up to 4m wide and 2.3m deep). The only way into and out from the stones was from the north, across an 8m-wide causeway, and the best view of what was happening inside would probably have been from the surrounding bank.

The surviving standing stones, stumps and concrete markers outline an oval that was around 30m in diameter. The modern markers indicate where archaeologists have found stone settings or holes. The stone circle is incomplete because there is no evidence for stones in at least one of the 12 settings. Timber posts possibly preceded some or all of the stones.

DEBUNKING THE DOLMEN

Just inside the original entrance to the henge is a low arrangement of stones. Early accounts reported a very large broad stone that lay towards the centre of the circle, and in his 1821 novel *The Pirate*, Sir Walter Scott encouraged the idea that the early Orcadians used it as an altar for human sacrifice. When the site came into state

Above: The Stones of Stenness from the air, with Structure 8 from Barnhouse village visible beyond. Approaching Stenness from the road you cross the line of the massive bank and ditch (now ploughed out), something the Neolithic builders would never have intended.

Below: Originally there were 12 standing stones at Stenness; today four remain. The remains of the 'dolmen' are visible in the foreground.

care in 1906, a 'dolmen' (a flat stone supported by vertical stones) was reconstructed in keeping with the interpretation of what had originally existed.

The 'dolmen' was removed in the mid-1970s, but this earlier reconstruction destroyed any surviving evidence of the original form. Archaeologists now think that three stones defined two sides of a narrow space. This interpretation begins to make more sense if we look at use of the henge in prehistoric times.

CEREMONIAL USE

The focus of the interior of the Stones of Stenness is a large, still-visible hearth, which an earlier hearth and timber upright would have preceded. The archaeologist Colin Richards argues that the first hearth came from the central area of Barnhouse; in other words, that the people of Barnhouse moved it here because of the special symbolism attached to hearths in general and this hearth in particular.

Above: The Grant family, photographed in 1909 next to the 'dolmen'.

That the hearth was significant can be seen from the line of features that marked the approach to it. Between the hearth and the entrance was a paved path, two stone settings, a setting that was apparently for another hearth, and the uprights of the 'dolmen'. The impression is, therefore, of a structured space to which access could be restricted but which those immediately outside the ditch could also view. We must imagine a large fire illuminating fingers of stone, as well as the sounds of people and musical instruments. Pottery and animal bones tell us that Neolithic visitors cooked and ate plenty of food at the site. Our best guess is that they were involved in activities and ceremonies that celebrated the relationship between living and past communities.

THE STONES OF STENNESS: BETWEEN THE HENGES

Stenness is a well-deserved name, for it comes from the Old Norse *Stein-nes*, meaning 'stone promontory'. In Neolithic times there would have been even more stones than we see today, including further standing stones, a second settlement and possibly other tombs. Archaeologists believe that these groups of standing stones encouraged people to move in certain directions through the landscape, between ceremonial sites and settlements.

THE WATCHSTONE

Below: The Watchstone stands at the very tip of the Stenness peninsula.

The Watchstone is the sole remaining sentinel that stands on the Stenness side of the causeway. Located a short distance north-west of the Stones of Stenness, the Watchstone is more than 5.6m high. It originally had a partner stone, which stood about 12.8m to the south–south-west, its stump found during roadworks in 1930. It is possible, therefore, that this stone and the Watchstone once marked the approach to the Ness of Brodgar, the promontory to the north of the causeway.

THE ODIN STONE

The Odin Stone was a standing stone with a hole in it, around which later local myths and traditions evolved. A farmer destroyed the stone in 1814, so we are reliant on antiquarian accounts and drawings for where it stood and what form it took. Excavations in the 1990s, just to the north of the Stones of Stenness, found evidence for not one but three stone settings, at least one with a possible timber predecessor. We think the southernmost of these is probably where the Odin Stone stood. An 18th-century drawing shows it surrounded by a small mound.

NESS OF BRODGAR SETTLEMENT

From the Stones of Stenness you can see how the modern bungalow at Lochview sits on an extensive mound. Since 2003, geophysical surveying and small-scale archaeological excavations have demonstrated that this mound comprises midden, midden-enhanced soils and a mass of early prehistoric domestic and ceremonial structures, including possible chambered tombs. Complex archaeology fills most of the ploughed fields in front of and behind the bungalow.

Archaeologists still have much to learn about this very exciting new discovery, which includes a well-built structure similar to Barnhouse's House 2. The proximity of these two settlements raises many questions about the relationship of their inhabitants to each other and to the ceremonial centres that developed around them.

Above: An 18th-century sketch of the Odin Stone, destroyed in 1814. The hole in the stone inspired a number of local traditions. Young people, for example, sealed their love by clasping hands through the hole.

Below: Two standing stones stand in the privately owned garden of the cottage at Lochview.

Left: Archaeological excavations at the Ness of Brodgar.

THE RING OF BRODGAR

The Ring of Brodgar is one of the most spectacular and well-preserved prehistoric monuments in the British Isles. A near perfect circle, 36 out of up to 60 original stones survive. Thirteen of these were re-erected shortly after the monument came into state care in 1906, and the same number survive as stumps only.

Above: The Ring of Brodgar from the air.

THE HENGE AND STONE CIRCLE

In contrast to the small henge at Stenness, with its single entrance, the Ring of Brodgar is one of the largest of all Neolithic henges, measuring 130m in diameter including its ditch, and has two causeways. Curiously, however, this henge seems to lack an outer bank, although there is the slight hint of an outer lip at one point. Accounts of the site go back to 1529, but only one such report mentions a bank. In 1973 archaeologists excavated three narrow trenches at the Ring – its only scientific exploration to date – but also found no evidence for a bank. Some of the material from the ditch presumably went to form the internal platform, but where the rest of it went remains a mystery. One possibility is that it was used to build some of the surrounding mounds.

The ring of stones itself is 104m in diameter. We do not know if the Neolithic builders ever finished erecting the 60 stones, but there would certainly have been space for them. We are also ignorant about what was in the centre. A 19th-century report of rapacious turf stripping from the site may well mean that much archaeological evidence has been lost. Archaeologists can make out little from geophysical surveying, and the area remains unexcavated.

Above: Excavations of the rock-cut ditch surrounding the Ring show that it was originally about 10m wide and 3.4m deep, with steeper sides than today.

Opposite: Of the surviving stones at the Ring, some lie where they fell or were pushed while others were re-erected by the Edwardians. One stone (the first smaller picture, opposite) was split by lightning in 1980. The rest have stood the test of time.

DATE AND FUNCTION

In the absence of useful scientific dates, our best guess is that the early Orcadians constructed this henge sometime between 4,500 and 4,000 years ago. This would make it slightly later than the Stones of Stenness, which is perhaps the earliest henge in the British Isles. Like Stenness, archaeologists think that the building and use of the Ring of Brodgar fulfilled a social and ceremonial function, probably associated with the commemoration of the dead. In contrast to Stenness, however, Brodgar is much more prominent and open to public view. At both sites activity extended well beyond the powerfully demarcated henge.

**THEY LOOK LIKE
AN ASSEMBLAGE OF
ANCIENT DRUIDS,
MYSTERIOUSLY STERN
AND INVINCIBLY
SILENT AND SHAGGY.**

The Scottish geologist
Hugh Miller, on his visit to
the Ring of Brodgar in 1846.

THE RING OF BRODGAR: A CEREMONIAL LANDSCAPE

Many visitors today first recognise the Ring of Brodgar for its 'natural' qualities, although humans have stamped their mark all over this landscape. The Ring of Brodgar is not just a stone circle and henge but the focus for other standing stones and many Neolithic and Bronze Age burial mounds that survive on both sides of the modern road passing the Ring.

EXPLORING THE TERRAIN

You can walk all around the site, but it will help to protect this fragile area if you keep to the mown paths and do not climb the mounds. From the Ring you can take a circular route through land owned by the RSPB, or, if on foot from the Stones of Stenness, you can join the path just north of Brodgar Farm. Allow around an hour to enjoy this route, which passes along the shores of the Loch of Stenness, providing access to the wildlife as well as very different views of how the monuments sit in the landscape.

Above: Frost covers the ditch around the Ring of Brodgar, with the Loch of Harray providing a peaceful backdrop.

Opposite: A lapwing (top) and a yellow bumblebee, two of the many non-human visitors to the area around the Ring.

NATURE CONSERVATION

Maintaining the Ring of Brodgar involves keeping its vegetation as natural as possible and managing the grass to encourage wild flowers and breeding birds. Since 2001 the RSPB have managed the farmland encircling the site. RSPB work includes managing a semi-natural wetland to the north of the Ring to encourage more breeding waders and wintering wildfowl, and ensuring that the arable area immediately outside the Ring promotes farmland biodiversity.

Regular avian visitors to the area include waders, skylarks, finches, buntings and hen harriers. Animal and insect life is abundant too, from brown hares to great yellow bumblebees. The arable weeds that grow in the area are ones which our ancestors would recognise. They include purple ramping fumitory and the edible fat hen. This vegetation gives us an idea of how the land looked in Neolithic times. As today, there would have been primroses in the spring and wild orchids, heather and bell heather during the summer months.

MONUMENTS AROUND THE RING OF BRODGAR

Around the Ring of Brodgar are at least 13 prehistoric burial mounds and a stone setting. The most recent may date to 3,500 years ago, but the earliest may pre-date the Ring and help to explain its existence. Their number, scale and diversity tell us that people regarded the area as important for a long time, and continued to use the Ring as a focus for ceremonial activities. Besides the mounds listed here, at least nine small mounds lie to the south of the Ring, from where none of them looks particularly impressive. But keep an eye out for them on the RSPB walk (see pages 36–37), when one grouping makes a very impressive mark on the skyline. Some appear disturbed but we have no reports of discoveries.

Below: Salt Knowe (on the left) rises above the fields to the south-west of the Ring of Brodgar (on the right). The abundance of monuments around the Ring indicates that this was a very special place for Orkney's Neolithic and Early Bronze-Age inhabitants.

COMET STONE

The Comet Stone is a 1.75m-high standing stone that lies to the south-east of the Ring. It may well have originally been part of a group of standing stones, since nearby two stumps rise from the low mound it stands on. Look out for the low bank that runs from the south towards the mound and then on to Plumcake Mound – an example of siting later field boundaries on existing features in the landscape.

SALT KNOWE

This massive mound, measuring 40m by 6m, is comparable in scale to Maeshowe and may well enclose another chambered tomb. A large slab on the top is probably part of a Bronze Age burial cist built into the mound.

PLUMCAKE MOUND

Named for its shape, Plumcake Mound is slightly smaller than the nearby Fresh Knowe. When the antiquarians James Farrer and George Petrie dug the mound in 1854 they found two stone cists. One contained a decorated steatite, or soapstone, urn (right), the other a pottery urn, both with cremated human remains.

SOUTH MOUND

While the form of this mound shows that it has been disturbed, we have no reports of discoveries. If you look carefully, you can see the line of an old track that ran between South Mound and the Ring of Brodgar.

FRESH KNOWE

Farrer disturbed this mound in 1853 when he dug a trench right across the middle of it. He observed the mound had been carefully constructed, but that was the extent of his reporting. Fresh Knowe's elliptical shape suggests that it might be an earlier Neolithic barrow that pre-dates the Ring.

THE RING OF BOOKAN – A THIRD CEREMONIAL FOCUS?

North-west from the Ring of Brodgar, and concealed just behind the brow of the hill, is the Ring of Bookan. Here a massive ditch, 13m wide and at least 2m deep, encloses a central area which appears at one time to have included a chamber. A large mound called Skae Frue sits on the slope beneath the Ring of Bookan. In the mid-19th century antiquarians found three cists containing skeletons in this mound.

Between the Ring of Bookan and the Ring of Brodgar are a host of interesting archaeological sites. The majority are visible from the Ring of Brodgar or the road, but recent geophysical surveys have illuminated the variety and extent of the hidden archaeology that also lies here.

DYKE O'SEAN

The Dyke o'Sean is an irregular earthen mound that snakes its way between the lochs of Harray and Stenness. Nowadays a modern boundary between the parishes of Stenness and Sandwick, during the Early Bronze Age (around 4,500 years ago) there was a move towards the enclosure of land, and the dyke may relate to such land divisions.

Above: The Ring of Bookan, an earthen circle thought to have been used by Neolithic people as a further ceremonial site.

There is no formal public access to the sites we describe here. Information is provided to help you interpret what you can see from the Ring of Brodgar or the road, and to help you better understand the landscape as a whole. Please remember to respect land in private ownership and to follow the Scottish Outdoor Access code (www.outdooraccess-scotland.com).

WASBISTER HOUSE

This house is difficult to see on the ground because it only survives as the low footings of two conjoined circular structures. To the surprise of archaeologists, however, geophysical surveying has revealed that Wasbister house sits within four hectares of fields and other settlement remains. The house may be Bronze Age, but the possibility of another Neolithic settlement has yet to be ruled out.

WASBISTER BARROW

Like the upstanding Wasbister house, Wasbister disc barrow is a rare survival, despite being a very slight feature. It consists of an enclosing ditch and bank, 30m in diameter, surrounding a revetted, circular mound which is 15m in diameter. It is possible that a burial cist would have been at its centre.

BOOKAN CHAMBERED CAIRN

This cairn, with its commanding views over the Brodgar peninsula, survives as a low, disturbed mound. In 2002 the archaeologist Nick Card excavated the site to advance the knowledge gained from Farrer and Petrie's 1861 excavations. We now know that the cairn had a far more complicated history of development than Farrer recognised, that it is late Neolithic in date and that its appearance was embellished towards the end of its development. Near the chambered cairn are three mounds, two of which we think are prehistoric burial cairns (the third being a modern quarry mound).

Above: An aerial photograph of the Ring of Bookan in its wider landscape, taken in the 1960s.

Left: (1) The Dyke o'Sean; **(2)** Wasbister barrow; and **(3)** Wasbister house.

A PLACE THAT TOUCHES THE HEART...
A CLUSTER OF HOUSES WHERE WE CAN SEE
THAT PEOPLE MOVED AND LIVED AND LOVED.

George Mackay Brown, *Portrait of Orkney* (1981)

SKARA BRAE VILLAGE

kara Brae is the best-preserved prehistoric farming settlement in northern Europe. It was continuously inhabited for around 600 years, from approximately 3100 BC to 2500 BC. The village survived because its construction is largely subterranean and because sand sealed it shortly after its abandonment. This wonderful site has its own guidebook, so the aim here is to highlight what is special about the place and how it helps us to understand the Maeshowe area.

BURIAL AND DISCOVERY

Skara Brae was originally built next to a small inland loch. Over the centuries the land between it and the sea disappeared because of coastal erosion. The village was then buried underneath sand dunes. But this was no Orcadian Pompeii – people did not run from their houses as the sand engulfed them. The burial of the site was a gradual process that began after the people who lived here moved on somewhere else.

In 1850 the Victorians discovered the first house after a storm stripped the grass from the dunes. Curious antiquarians explored the site, but its present appearance is largely a direct consequence of its clearance between 1928 and 1930 by the archaeologist Gordon Childe. Childe's primary motivation was to present the site to the public after it came into state care.

DIFFERENT PHASES

We will never know how large the settlement at Skara Brae was, nor can we understand its full and complex history. All the evidence, however, suggests a community of people who worked and lived closely together. In simple terms, we can divide the visible remains into two phases. The first phase comprised freestanding buildings, which the buildings of the second phase largely destroyed and now obscure.

While houses of both phases share the same cross-shaped arrangement, those from the later phase are slightly larger and were deliberately built into midden, which provided more shelter and made construction easier. Another difference is that the 'beds' in houses from the second phase project from the walls instead of being built into them.

Above top: House 8 at Skara Brae, with the Bay of Skaill in the background.

Above: Gordon Childe (bottom left), excavating at Skara Brae in the late 1920s.

Opposite: The entranceway for House 7 at Skara Brae. Covered passages led to and from individual houses in the village, providing shelter from the elements. Skeletal remains show that Neolithic people's average height was only about 6cm shorter than today, so the villagers must have crouched along the low passages.

SKARA BRAE: UNDERSTANDING THE BUILDINGS

The well-preserved remains of Skara Brae help us to imagine what the ploughed-out settlement at Barnhouse once looked like. A far better range of artefacts has survived at Skara Brae than at Barnhouse. This is not to suggest that the architecture of the villages, or the people who lived in them, was identical. Nonetheless, there are similarities in the architecture and the use of buildings that hint at common beliefs.

HOUSE 9

House 9 is a good example of one of the freestanding houses from the first phase of building at Skara Brae, with its 'beds' built into the core of the wall. It is similar to House 3 at Barnhouse. The houses from the earlier building phase are less well-preserved than those that came later. The builders of these later dwellings robbed houses – such as House 9 – for materials, which they reused in their new constructions.

HOUSE I

House I is later than House 9, and illustrates the classic arrangement of boxes and a dresser around a central hearth. From Barnhouse we know that people moved in an anti-clockwise direction around the hearth. Among other things, this means they avoided the ash that they usually emptied to their left. Around the hearth are stone querns for grinding cereals, as well as tanks for food storage.

A rich collection of objects survives from Skara Brae, including these stone containers.

These beautifully carved stone objects may have been used in religious ceremonies.

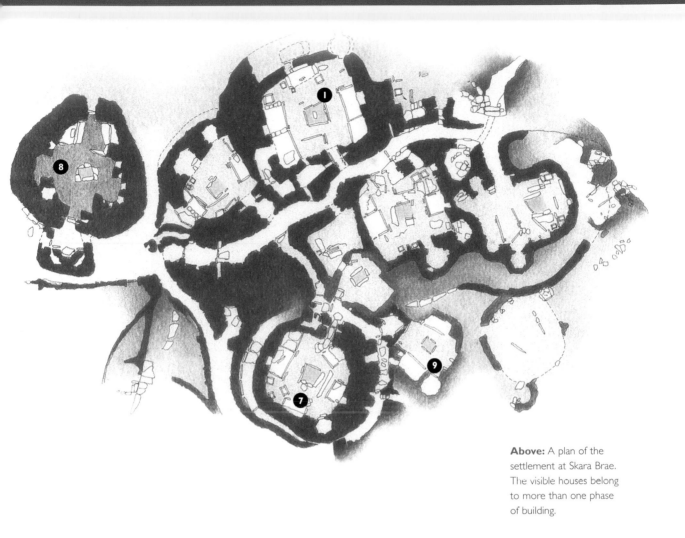

Above: A plan of the settlement at Skara Brae. The visible houses belong to more than one phase of building.

HOUSE 7

House 7 stands apart from the rest of the Skara Brae settlement in every sense, including the fine nature of its architecture, the high level of its carved stone decoration and the remains of two women found buried beneath its floor. All this evidence suggests that it had a specialised ritual function. The distinctive qualities and use of this building evoke House 2 at Barnhouse.

HOUSE 8

The freestanding House 8 is set apart from the other buildings. Inside it was much evidence for the working of chert, a flint-like stone from which prehistoric tools were made. House 8 reminds us of House 6 at Barnhouse, which was lived in but was also the focus of stone-working. Like House 8 at Skara Brae, the orientation of Barnhouse's House 6 singles it out as different from the other houses.

THE STORY OF
NEOLITHIC
ORKNEY

THE ORKNEY IMAGINATION IS HAUNTED BY TIME.

George Mackay Brown, *The Orkney Tapestry* (1969)

STONE SOCIETIES

The Neolithic people who lived on Orkney between 5,000 and 3,500 years ago were not the islands' first inhabitants. They were, however, the first to move away from a nomadic lifestyle and settle in small agricultural communities. It was these communities who built the houses, tombs, henges and standing stones that survive today.

Nature blessed Orkney and its Neolithic inhabitants with a geological mantle of Old Red Sandstone that readily forms plentiful, regular-shaped slabs to build with. So many prehistoric houses survive in Orkney because people quickly mastered the art of drystone masonry, learning to square the edges and smooth the surfaces of stones, and to carefully rebate them too, as at Maeshowe.

Many different groups of sandstone are present in the Stones of Stenness and the Ring of Brodgar, possibly from different sources. Transporting the stones with ropes and timber rollers over land, or on boats across the lochs, must have been a phenomenal communal exercise involving many hands. We can imagine the shared preparation of food and feasting along the way – processes which we certainly know took place at the stone circles themselves.

The creation of the Neolithic monuments on Orkney represents more than feats of engineering. It took perhaps as many as 80,000 man-hours to build the Ring of Brodgar or Maeshowe, and up to 50,000 man-hours to erect the Stones of Stenness. It is unlikely that any of these structures would have been the achievement of a village community acting on its own. There is no evidence of a centralised authority in Orkney, but the creation and use of the monuments may reflect a highly competitive society in which certain dominant groups could persuade others with shared beliefs or family ties to act together.

Below: The dry-stone walls at Skara Brae are one example of the accomplished building skills of the inhabitants.

Above: This 1906 photograph taken during the re-erection of one of the stones at Stenness conveys the effort involved in moving such big stones.

This stone walked through the hills

Between cornstalk and fish.

What, the men groaned and bled

Clearing a way for the Stones?

One skull, in truth,

Has been laid bare by the eagles.

I tell you, the men danced.

They stretched their mouths with praise, laughter.

George Mackay Brown,
Brodgar Poems (1992)

This page: Cliffs beyond Skara Brae, facing the Atlantic swell. The easy-to-work sandstone that forms these cliffs is also readily available on the beach by Skara Brae itself.

Opposite: An artist's impression of how a stone circle was built, with a wooden frame to help raise each stone.

Previous pages: The Stones of Stenness at sunset, looking across the Loch of Stenness.

MARKING TIME AND PLACE

Tombs, henges, stone circles and other massive structures are among the earliest attempts by our ancestors to physically mark or alter the surface of the earth. The Neolithic stonemasons of Orkney built to impress through physical form, texture, scale and architectural finesse. From certain viewpoints some of their monuments are virtually invisible, but others suddenly rise out of the landscape to confront you with their presence.

The builders thought carefully about how to achieve such effects, including how the monuments looked from the water. The henge, platform and standing stones at the Ring of Brodgar, for instance, form a prominent landscape feature, particularly if seen from the Loch of Harray side. It is also possible that the builders tried to mimic the strong features of the surrounding landscape. The shape of Maeshowe, for example, reflects the Hills of Hoy, while the henge ditches resemble the lochs, effectively creating islands within islands.

PURPOSE AND MOVEMENT

For tombs and henges, as well as villages, social practice and architecture conditioned where people could go, what they might do and what they experienced. Considerable effort went into separating spaces from each other and placing restrictions on who might enter them, whether it was the deep, inner recesses of Maeshowe or the interior of a henge.

Opposite: This drawing by John Cleveley in 1772 shows the relationship between the Stones of Stenness (in the foreground), the Odin Stone (to the right), the Watchstone (middle) and the Ring of Brodgar (in the distance).

Below: Maeshowe with the Hills of Hoy behind. Was the mound a conscious attempt to imitate these natural forms?

Henges – places for ritual, theatre and spectacle – were constructed to direct and control the movement of people. The alignment of the henge entrances suggests the importance of directing people along the long axis of the promontories, between Stenness to the south and the Ring of Bookan to the north. Everyone who passed this way would have encountered the inhabitants of Barnhouse and those who lived on the narrow spit of land at Ness of Brodgar.

VILLAGE BUILDINGS

Barnhouse and Skara Brae also show the importance of form, orientation and location for the Neolithic Orcadians. While we can never know how these early folk viewed the world, the evidence suggests that they were sensitive to both the growing seasons and the cycles of the moon and the sun. Aspects of these beliefs are apparent in their settlement layouts and plans of houses. It is possible, for example, that the cross-shaped layout of a typical Neolithic house reflects how its inhabitants viewed the world, with each side of the building embodying the key points in the annual cycle governing agriculture and social practices.

At Barnhouse, the buildings fall into an inner and outer ring, defined by a sophisticated system of connecting drains. Notions of impurity and pollution may explain this separation. The buildings in these rings had different uses. The outer ring – incorporating the highly unusual structure of House 2 – was close to the central area with its monumental open hearth, where eating took place. The inner ring had greater access to the open area to the south, where there is evidence for craft-working activities.

Above: The cross-shaped layout of House 3 at Barnhouse village is discernible in this photograph.

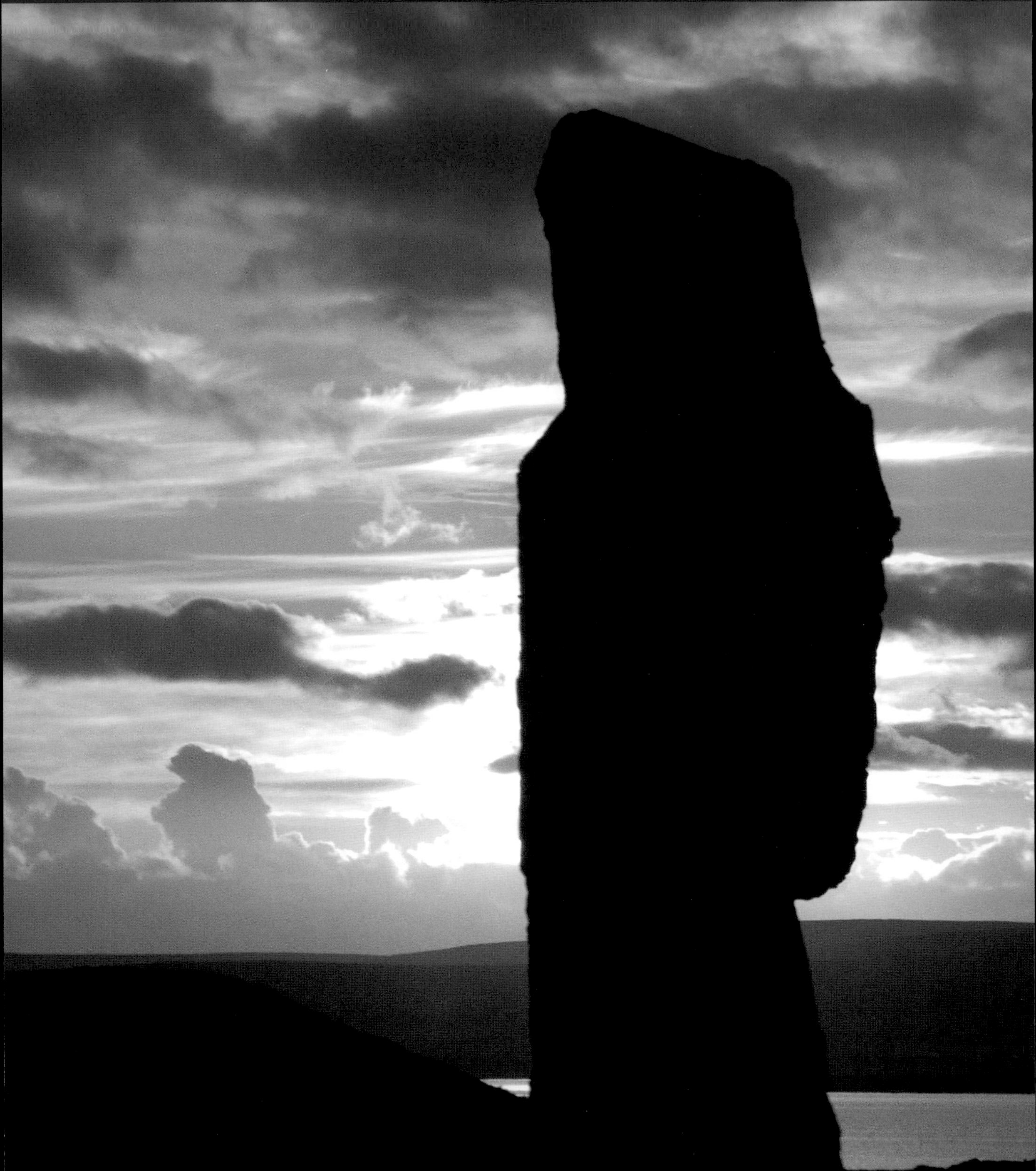

THE LIVING AND THE DEAD

There is increasing evidence that the bodies of ancestors played an important part in the daily life of Scotland's prehistoric peoples. These were folk who circulated bones in and out of chambered tombs and laid their dead under houses. In the Western Isles, for example, there is evidence that Bronze-Age people circulated mummified bodies for generations before burying them under their houses.

A SENSE OF BELONGING

The assertion of ancestral connections to a particular place was common to most prehistoric societies, including Neolithic Orkney. Communal tombs were one visible way of associating a local community with a given area, weaving the remains of the dead into the fabric of daily life. The way people moved and recycled hearthstones suggests that these, too, were closely associated with particular groups of people.

Standing stones may also have been associated with individuals, as both iconic representations of the places they came from and the people who transported them. If Neolithic people associated the anthropomorphic forms of standing stones with their ancestors, then lines of ancestry were fused within the landscape, which became a place for mapping genealogies and evoking memories. Several stone maceheads originally came from the area around the Odin Stone (see page 33) and its fellow standing stones. Maceheads are usually associated with burials – this strengthens the argument that some standing stones could be linked with the dead.

Above: Parallels between places for the living and the dead are reflected throughout Orkney. For example, there are clear architectural links between the types of dwelling at Knap of Howar on Papa Westray (above top) and the chambered cairn, or tomb, at Midhowe on Rousay (above).

Opposite: The setting sun gives this standing stone at the Ring of Brodgar a particularly human-like outline. It is possible that such stones were iconic representations of individuals.

Below: The carvings on this stone found at Skara Brae possibly held a deeply symbolic meaning for the villagers.

SHARED ARCHITECTURE

Parallels in the architecture of Orcadian Late Neolithic houses and Maeshowe-type tombs and henges reinforce this sense of an ever-present relationship between the living and the dead. Just as at Barnhouse the design and orientation of later houses may have reflected daily and annual life cycles, so Maeshowe itself is intimately associated with the birth of each new year.

The outer enclosure of Barnhouse's Structure 8 faces Maeshowe, while the entrance to its internal building aligns on the midsummer sunset, the seasonal opposite of Maeshowe. Such references and oppositions surely carried great and intentional symbolic meaning. Similarly, carvings within the houses and tombs, often no more than light scratch marks, provide further links. Often scarcely noticeable, the very act of carving could carry the most meaning.

DAY-TO-DAY LIVING

From Skara Brae, Barnhouse and other settlements we can begin to construct a picture of some of the day-to-day realities of living in Neolithic Orkney. Unlike their mainland neighbours, ancient Orcadians were fortunate to have no animal predators and competitors to contend with, such as wolves and bears. Their main challenge was ensuring that food was available at all times, and especially when crops failed.

NATURAL RESOURCES

Cattle, sheep and pigs were more than a source of meat – they also provided milk, blood, skins, wool and bone for working into tools and other objects. When animals were slaughtered, evidence suggests that the messy process of butchery took place away from the main settlements.

Right: An artist's impression of how the interior of House 1 at Skara Brae might have looked.

Below: The hearth in House 7 at Skara Brae. Hearths were the focal point of Neolithic homes.

Orkney's Neolithic farmers could also fish, hunt and gather. In addition to fish and shellfish, the sea produced its bounty of beached whales and other marine mammals, which served as an excellent source of oil for lamps. Wild birds were also useful for meat, eggs and oil, while red deer, now extinct on Orkney, were an excellent source of leather, bone and antler for tools such as picks, as well as meat. Early Orcadians also cultivated cereals, such as barley and wheat, and collected hazelnuts, edible wild seeds and fruit, including crab apples and crowberries.

Analysis of pottery vessels suggests these people cooked plants and milk-related products in them. Bone and stone tools suggest a wide range of craft activities took place, including leather-, stone- and woodworking. Not all the products are obviously utilitarian: some would have been used in games while others are likely to have had ritual significance.

Above and below: Stone axe-heads and bone necklaces, both from Skara Brae.

HEARTHS AND HEALTH

Hearths were a source of light and warmth and the focus of Neolithic houses. Outside the home, hearths played a role in communal feasting and possibly in symbolic purification at the entrance to special places. A range of materials might keep the hearths burning, including turf, animal dung, dried seaweed and heather.

We have no evidence for what Neolithic peoples wore – presumably leathers, skins and felted fabrics. We know that bone pins, beads and pendants formed adornments. It is possible that people used coloured pigments to decorate their bodies and clothes, along with feathers, another useful source of insulation.

Knowledge of the benefits and dangers of certain plants will have developed from earliest times. For instance, a large collection of a type of puffball found at Skara Brae suggests that its inhabitants recognised the plant's medicinal value in helping to clot blood.

Right: Puffballs (*Bovista nigrescens*), a type of fungi found at Skara Brae. The villagers may well have applied puffballs to wounds as a blood-clotting agent.

BEYOND ORKNEY

Neolithic peoples throughout the British Isles had many practices in common. Activities included the burial of the dead in communal tombs, the erection of timber and stone circles, the construction of henges and the use of Grooved Ware – a distinctive form of pottery with incised and applied decoration.

Evidence from settlements, tombs and ceremonial sites provides patterns which bring us as close as we can be to what made our ancestors tick. What emerges is the shared sense of a way of doing things, and the suggestion that no distinction existed between 'ritual' and 'domestic' activities. Local circumstances transformed the expression of these common beliefs – notable, for example, was the development of different types of tomb architecture – yet some parts of the British Isles show evidence of particularly strong connections.

SEAFARING FOLK

Orkney's pivotal maritime location at the top of the British mainland may help to explain why we find strong links between its architecture, pottery and carvings and those elsewhere in the British Isles. No vessels survive from this time, but we should imagine skin boats capable of carrying people and animals.

There are particularly strong links between the architecture of Orkney's passage graves and the tombs in Ireland's Boyne Valley. Shared designs on Grooved Ware, ornate stone objects and the carvings embellishing tombs and houses reinforce this connection. While the Boyne Valley tombs are slightly earlier than the graves in Orkney – where communal burial lasts longer than elsewhere – Orcadian Grooved Ware is as early as any found in the British Isles. Similarly, no other henge in Britain predates the Stones of Stenness.

Orkney's links go in other directions, too, since henges have a predominantly eastern distribution in Britain. The discovery of exotic artefacts in settlements also speaks of distant connections. A good example is the pitchstone from Arran which lay near the large, central hearth at Barnhouse. A distinctive type of stone used to make tools, it is possible that the inhabitants displayed it at formal gatherings.

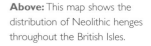

Orkney

circle henge
henge
possible henge

Boyne Valley

0 ___ 100 kilometres

Above: This map shows the distribution of Neolithic henges throughout the British Isles.

Opposite: Looking across Scapa Flow to the Hills of Hoy.

Above: Grooved Ware pottery from Skara Brae.

Below: The similarities between these two carved stones, one found at Pierowall on the Orkney island of Westray (left) and the other at Newgrange in Ireland, speak of shared practices and beliefs.

BEYOND BRITANNIA, WHERE THE
ENDLESS OCEANS OPEN, LIES ORKNEY.

Orosius, 5th century AD

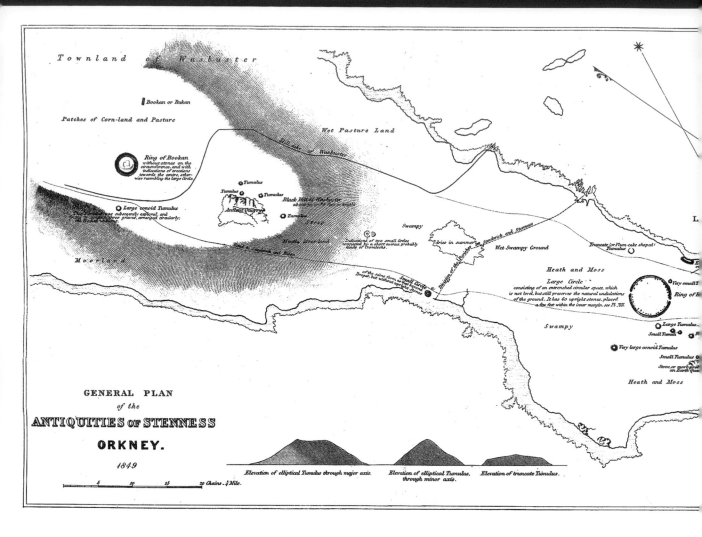

GENERAL PLAN
of the
ANTIQUITIES OF STENNESS
ORKNEY.
1849

FROM THEN TO NOW

In Neolithic and Early Bronze Age times the Maeshowe area of Orkney was a very special place. There came a point, however, when the use of the monuments changed. People stopped entering Maeshowe or using it for burial. They also altered or stopped their ceremonies at the Stones of Stenness. In contrast, the Ring of Brodgar, with its surrounding barrows, suggests a longer history of ritual activity.

The current evidence does not allow us to identify the area as particularly unusual in the millennia that follow, but we do know that the ancient burial places and standing stones continued to attract interest. A body of folklore developed to explain the monuments, such as tales of the trows (trolls) who lived in the mounds. In the 17th century, Oliver Cromwell's soldiers allegedly dug in Maeshowe, but found nothing.

We are better at noticing settlements from some periods than others, but it is likely that there was continuous habitation in the Maeshowe area. From the Bronze Age comes the evidence of the settlement at Wasbister, while in the Iron Age, around 2,000 years ago, brochs appeared on the promontories on either side

Above: In 1849 Captain F.W.L. Thomas conducted a survey of the monuments on the Brodgar peninsula. His map shows what some of these sites looked like before archaeologists investigated them or farmers ploughed them away. It also shows how today's landscape differs in terms of its vegetation, field boundaries and roads.

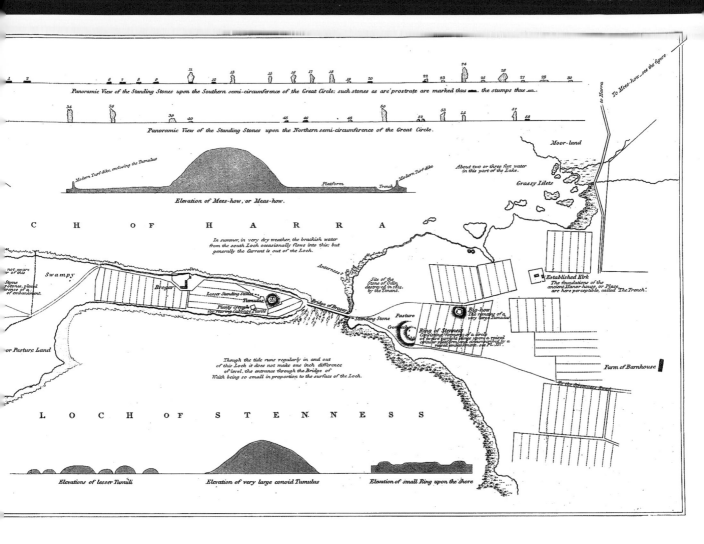

Panoramic View of the Standing Stones upon the Southern semi-circumference of the Great Circle; such stones as are prostrate are marked thus ▬, the stumps thus ▬.

Panoramic View of the Standing Stones upon the Northern semi-circumference of the Great Circle.

of what is now the Bridge of Brodgar. South-east from the Stones of Stenness you can see the mound at Big Howe, which may well contain the remains of one of these massive stone towers and its associated external settlements. People probably lived here well into the Pictish period (around AD 300 to 900).

The next significant evidence for human activity in the Maeshowe area comes more than 1,000 years later, from the Norse. In addition to Maeshowe, the Norse carved runes on stones around the Brodgar area. They also left a hoard of Viking silver ring-money, probably dating from the 9th or 10th centuries, in Salt Knowe or Freshwater Knowe. The silver was discovered some time before 1700 but is now lost. The parish church at Stenness may have its origins in the late Norse period. Such churches were usually built at estate centres, where there would also be an important house and a farm. The foundations of a 'palace' at Stenness, to the south-east of the church, were still visible in 1849.

Farming dominates the area's recent history. The fields and run-rigs (cultivation strips) seen on Captain Thomas's plan (above) still show on today's geophysical surveys of the area, but later field patterns now mask them. The Neolithic monuments – Orkney's ancient treasury – are once more the focus of attention, for we travel from around the world to visit them.

Above: Stenness parish church (top) and sheep and arable farming near Maeshowe.

THE ROOTS OF OUR UNDERSTANDING

The task of unpicking the landscape around Maeshowe begins with the records left us by antiquarians, those 17th- to 19th-century forerunners of modern archaeologists who sought to understand the ancient world.

On the one hand, we are lucky because the Maeshowe area attracted considerable antiquarian interest, and people such as James Farrer and George Petrie left plans, drawings and accounts of their work. In addition, in the 1780s a number of scientific expeditions called into Orkney on their way to Iceland. Their surveys and sketches are systematic and show a good eye for detail.

On the other hand, most antiquarians' excavation techniques were very poor, and the quality of their records is often so bad that it is impossible to interpret their findings very closely. Their efforts provide some important clues and alert us to the archaeological possibilities of the monuments and landscape in Orkney's World Heritage area, but the precision that today's archaeologists require is totally lacking.

Right: In 1772 the antiquarian Sir Joseph Banks visited Orkney on his way to Iceland. Banks' team carried out excavation and survey work, and produced this 'Plan of the Circle of Loda' (the Ring of Brodgar).

Below: This late 18th-century painting of the Ring of Brodgar includes the note, made by the artist, 'A druidical circle of 150 yards diameter'.

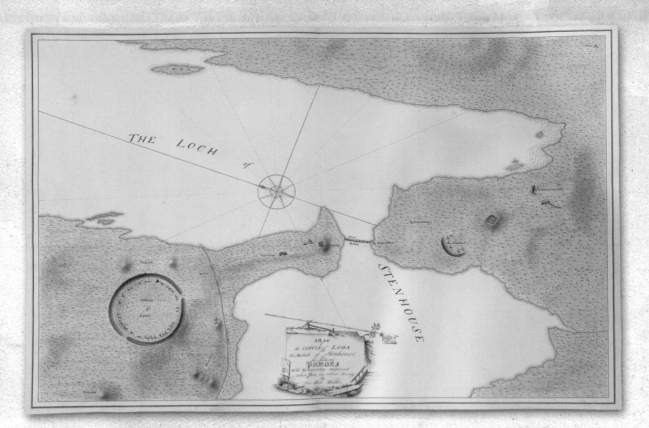

MODERN DISCOVERIES

Over the course of the 20th century our knowledge of archaeology and prehistory improved dramatically, allowing us to make firmer assumptions about the Neolithic monuments in Orkney and elsewhere. Today, we take it for granted that the buildings that make up the Orkney World Heritage Site date from the Neolithic period, more than 5,000 years ago, but when Gordon Childe dug Skara Brae in the 1920s he thought it was Pictish – dating from around 1,300 years ago – rather than Neolithic. Even in the 1930s, when Childe realised he was wrong, the dates of the Neolithic period were still guesswork.

Above: Archaeologists (including Gordon Childe, top left) at work at Maeshowe in the mid-1950s. Their trench runs from the ditch, across the platform and up into the mound.

RADIOCARBON REVOLUTION

The biggest leap forward in understanding prehistoric buildings and artefacts came with the radiocarbon revolution of the 1950s, allowing for the scientific dating of archaeological events. Our knowledge about Orkney's Neolithic monuments is still limited, however, and any timeline that reflects the development of the buildings must be treated with caution. The present dates for the World Heritage Site all derive from small-scale excavations in the 1970s. In the surrounding area, the only modern, large-scale excavations are those at Barnhouse in the 1980s.

Because there has been so little excavation to modern standards, we often also lack the subtleties of detail and sequence that might enable us to imagine and compare what individual places might have looked like at given times. We still do not know, for example, whether the ditches and banks of the henges predate the stone circles – and we have yet to discover what predates the stone circles themselves. Our present lenses only allow us to see major changes in the material evidence and the societies that produced it.

GEOPHYSICAL SURVEYS

Geophysical surveying is a tool that archaeologists use to see what is beneath the ground without disturbing anything. It compresses the features of geological and human history and so requires careful interpretation, which can often be only fully understood through excavation. The occasional glimpses of finer detail humble archaeologists with the bewildering complexities they present.

Surveys have taken place over much of the Maeshowe area, followed by some excavation. This work confirms what a busy and significant place it once was, but more research still needs to be done. Our knowledge and understanding, like the landscape around us, is constantly changing.

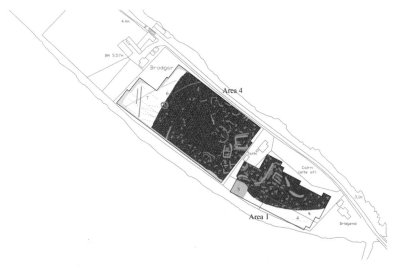

Left: A plan showing how archaeologists have interpreted the findings from a geophysical survey conducted in the Ness of Brodgar area.

Maeshowe and the other monuments that make up the Heart of
Neolithic Orkney are among nearly 40 Historic Scotland sites
on Orkney, a selection of which is shown below.

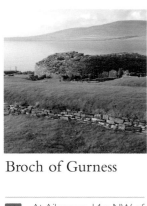   

Broch of Gurness

↗ At Aikerness, 14m NW of Kirkwall on the A966

🕐 Open summer only

📞 01856 751414

🚗 Approx 15 miles from Maeshowe

Facilities
P 🚌 🍴 🛍 £

Unstan Chambered Cairn

↗ About 3.5m NNE of Stromness on the A965

🕐 Open all year

📞 01856 841815 (Skara Brae)

🚗 Approx 5 miles from Maeshowe

Brough of Birsay

↗ On a tidal island at Birsay, 20m NW of Kirkwall off the A966. Check tide tables at Skara Brae

🕐 Open when tides permit, mid-June to 30 Sept.

📞 01856 841815 (Skara Brae)

🚗 Approx 14 miles from Maeshowe

Facilities
P 🍴 🛍 £

Midhowe Chambered Cairn

↗ On the island of Rousay on the B9064, 5m from pier

🕐 Open all year

📞 01856 841815 (Skara Brae)

🚗 Approx 21 miles from Maeshowe

For more information on all Historic Scotland sites, visit **www.historic-scotland.gov.uk**
To order tickets and a wide range of gifts, visit **www.historic-scotland.gov.uk/shop**

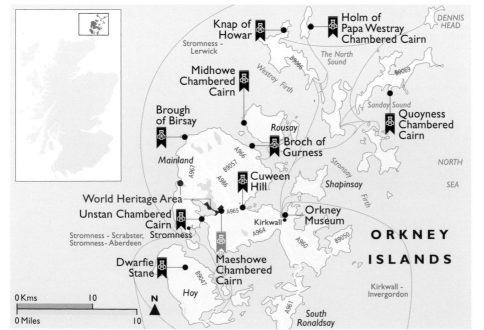

Key to facilities

Admission charge	£
Bus/coach parking	🚌
Car parking	P
Interpretive display	🍴
Picnic area	🪑
Reasonable wheelchair access	♿
Shop	🛍
Toilets	🚻
Visitor centre	ℹ

Strong footwear recommended at Brough of Birsay and Midhowe Chambered Cairn